W9-CFK-753

How *Annie* Made It to the Stage

Jeri Freedman

Cavendish Square

New York

Published in 2019 by Cavendish Square Publishing, LLC
243 5th Avenue, Suite 136, New York, NY 10016

Copyright © 2019 by Cavendish Square Publishing, LLC

First Edition

Library of Congress Cataloging-in-Publication Data

Names: Freedman, Jeri, author.
Title: How Annie made it to the stage / Jeri Freedman.
Description: New York : Cavendish Square, 2019. | Series: Getting to Broadway | Includes bibliographical references and index. | Audience: Grades 7-12.
Identifiers: LCCN 2017048028 (print) | LCCN 2017053509 (ebook) | ISBN 9781502634993 (library bound) | ISBN 9781502635013 (pbk.) | ISBN 9781502635006 (ebook)
Subjects: LCSH: Strouse, Charles. Annie--Juvenile literature. | Charnin, Martin. Annie--Juvenile literature. | Meehan, Thomas. Annie--Juvenile literature. | Gray, Harold, 1894-1968. Little Orphan Annie--Juvenile literature.
Classification: LCC ML3930.S885 (ebook) | LCC ML3930.S885 F74 2018 (print) | DDC 792.6/42--dc23
LC record available at https://lccn.loc.gov/2017048028

Editorial Director: David McNamara
Editor: Tracey Maciejewski
Copy Editor: Rebecca Rohan
Associate Art Director: Amy Greenan
Designer: Lindsey Auten
Production Coordinator: Karol Szymczuk
Photo Research: J8 Media

Printed in the United States of America

Contents

Chapter 1

The Influences on *Annie*

Annie is a landmark play. It has made many contributions to musical theater. Among them is the song "Tomorrow," which is now a standard. The original play was staged more than two thousand times on Broadway. It spawned movies and has gone through several revivals. It helped to launch the careers of several actors, including Sarah Jessica Parker. Its greatest achievement was to restore the musical to prominence, opening the way for the staging of the greatest blockbusters ever performed.

Musical tastes turned during the 1960s and 1970s, taking audiences that had flocked to plays such as *Hello Dolly* and *Oklahoma!* with them. Rock music performed in the style of a revue took over. *Annie* revived the musical that followed the story of an individual character. Plays such as *Wicked* and *Phantom of the Opera* owe a debt to the play

Opposite: This stamp shows Annie and Sandy as they appeared in Harold Gray's original comic strip.

named for a young girl created for a comic strip. The ironic thing is that the beginnings of that character almost kept the play from being produced.

That character, Annie, is from the comic strip *Little Orphan Annie*, which was created by Harold Gray (1894–1968). The little orphan girl who is the title character has been a part of American culture since 1924. She has appeared in print, on radio, in the movies, and on Broadway.

Many of comic-strip Annie's characteristics were incorporated into the musical's Annie. The play's central character is a streetwise, self-reliant, resourceful girl, who, with a little help from her friend, businessman Daddy Warbucks, fights criminals who endanger America. However, Annie did not become Warbucks's adopted daughter in the comic strip as she does in the play. Instead, she remained independent and self-reliant, becoming involved in new adventures on those occasions when she visited Warbucks's home.

The play incorporated the characters of Annie and Daddy Warbucks from the comic strip but gave Annie's story a cute, upbeat turn, in contrast to the often political tone of the comic. In addition, the authors dropped two characters, Punjab and the Asp, from the story. In the 1930s, during the Great Depression, millions of people lost their wealth and jobs. Gray was very conservative in his views, believing in capitalism and admiring those who became wealthy through their own efforts. He supported big business and opposed labor unions, income taxes, and governmental regulation in American life. Although his views were conservative, Gray was sympathetic to immigrants, minorities, and the poor. He believed that all people should advance through their own efforts and hard work, without the government interfering in the process. He especially disliked President Franklin D. Roosevelt's New Deal program, which provided paid work for the unemployed, using government funds, and he frequently attacked Roosevelt in the strip. This produced a conundrum for the authors of the musical *Annie*. In the play, President Roosevelt calls upon Daddy Warbucks for help, which he provides. The authors had to reconcile Gray's Warbucks's negative attitude toward Roosevelt in the comic strip with their own version, which reflected their more liberal, humanistic view.

Another aspect of Annie that carried over from the comic to the stage was her indomitable spirit—she never gives up, no matter what obstacles she faces. What she lacks in resources, Annie makes up for with pluck. She represents the underdog, whom the audience wants to win despite the odds against her. Beyond that she represents courage in the face of unreasonable authority. Being a girl she has the appeal of cuteness, but instead of being passive, she is strong and determined, characteristics that made her popular in the 1930s—and in 1977 when the play was produced and the women's movement was promoting the vision of women as not just decorative but also strong.

Throughout the life of the strip, Annie was always involved in the affairs of the day. During World War II, Gray was a strong supporter of the Allies fighting Germany. In the comic and in visits to schools, he used Annie to

THE *LITTLE ORPHAN ANNIE* COMIC STRIP

Harold Gray's parents died in 1912 while he was still in school, so he had personal experience of what it was like to be on his own at a young age. Gray graduated from Purdue University in Lafayette, Indiana, in 1917 and worked for the *Chicago Tribune* newspaper. He left the paper in 1919 and became assistant to cartoonist Sidney Smith, who had a strip called *The Gumps* in the *New York Daily News*.

Gray began to formulate ideas for his own strip and pitched a number of ideas to Joseph Medill Patterson, editor of the *New York Daily News*. Gray finally won Patterson over in 1924 with the concept of a strip based on an orphan, Little Orphan Otto, an independent little boy who had a variety of adventures. Patterson liked the novelty of the idea, but he was trying to attract female readers, so he ordered Gray to make the little boy appealing to women. The result was a cute boy with curls. Patterson felt the character looked too girly for a boy hero, so he told Gray to make the character a girl instead.

Little Orphan Annie's name came from James Whitcomb Riley's well-known 1885 poem "Little Orphant Annie" (the poem contributed only the character's name). As a little girl with courage, fortitude, and ingenuity, Annie was a hit. The strip debuted in the

The *Little Orphan Annie* comic strip eventually appeared in newspapers around the country.

New York Daily News on August 5, 1924. Gray described Annie as "tougher than hell, with a heart of gold and a fast left, who can take care of herself because she has to." Many of Annie's signature characteristics were established from the beginning of the strip, including her red dress, her frizzy hair, and her dog, Sandy. Daddy Warbucks was a major figure in the comic strip as Annie's protector, and he often was a mouthpiece for Gray's conservative political views. Daddy Warbucks had two bodyguards/assistants with mystical powers: Punjab, a wizard from India, and the Asp.

encourage children to become Junior Commandos and help with the war effort. The Junior Commandos collected scrap metal, rubber, nylon, kitchen fats, and paper and gave these materials to the government, which used them in manufacturing goods for the war effort. For example, fats were used to make glycerin for use in medicines and nitroglycerin for explosives.

Large Following

In its heyday, the *Little Orphan Annie* strip appeared in hundreds of newspapers. When the New York newspaper deliverymen's strike occurred in 1945, New York Mayor Fiorello La Guardia read Annie's adventures on the radio for her fans. However, not everyone at the time was comfortable with the character of the tough, self-reliant girl. Gray said, "She's controversial, there's no question about that. But I keep her on the side of motherhood, honesty, and decency."

After Gray's death in 1968, the media syndicate that distributed the comic strip tried hiring several different artists to draw and write new *Little Orphan Annie* strips, but they failed to find favor with the public. Instead, the syndicate reran old strips until 1977, when a new incarnation of Little Orphan Annie, the musical *Annie*, whetted the public's appetite for new material. To meet the demand, the syndicate engaged Leonard Star to do the strip. He retired in 2000, but the strip ran for another ten years, being drawn by two other cartoonists. Annie changed over time as well, remaining relevant. In the 1970s, "Little Orphan" was dropped from the title of the comic strip, and this change transferred to the play. Eventually, she stopped wearing her signature red dress as well, switching to an outfit consisting of jeans and sneakers. Her enemies changed over the years as the villains in society changed from Nazis and gangsters to drug cartels and terrorists, but she continued to be a working-class girl—someone who represented the ordinary people, and who was the bane of bureaucrats and the pretentious. The comic strip continued to promote the ideals of self-reliance as well. People might need a bit of help from a well-off friend, such as Daddy Warbucks, but they didn't need government interference. The strip ended in 2010, a victim of the reduction in the size of print newspapers and the audience for newspaper comic strips.

Orphan Annie Radio Show

The first live performance version of *Little Orphan Annie* wasn't the Broadway musical. Rather it was the *Orphan Annie* radio show, which premiered on WGN/Chicago in 1930. (The radio show never used the term "Little" when referring to Annie.) The show was a hit. It moved to NBC's Blue Network in 1931 and began to air nationwide. It continued to be broadcast until 1942. In the 1930s, radio shows were performed live with actors reading from a script into a microphone as the performance was broadcast to avid listeners. It was similar to a play. The *Orphan Annie* radio show was a serial—what we would call a continuing story today. It was the first radio serial aimed at families, not just adults. The show was broadcast five days a week at 5:45, after children came home from school but before they went to bed, and it featured a new episode every day. The show was popular with both kids and adults. Annie in the show was far from being the cute little girl in the musical. She was tough, fighting criminals, pirates, and Nazis, providing exciting adventures for her audience. In the radio show, Annie solved mysteries with the help of Daddy Warbucks, her friend Joe Corntassel, and her faithful dog Sandy. Like the musical, it featured a catchy theme song.

PARENTAL PROTESTS

Some concerned parents objected to the *Orphan Annie* radio show. They felt that it overstimulated children. In 1933, mothers in Scarsdale, New York, held a protest, and a Minneapolis branch of the American Association of University Women and the Board of Managers of the Iowa Congress of Parents and Teachers adopted resolutions condemning *Orphan Annie* and other children's serials.

One of the sponsors of the show was Ovaltine, a malted cocoa-flavored powder for mixing with hot milk. Ovaltine encouraged the growth in the audience by providing them with a range of advertising premiums. Among the giveaways were *Little Orphan Annie* mugs for drinking Ovaltine, whistles, periscopes, and secret decoders, which listeners could use to decode a secret message given in some episodes. During most of the show's run, which lasted until 1942, Annie was played by actress Shirley Bell. In 1990, *Orphan Annie* was inducted into the National Radio Hall of Fame.

Radio actors from the 1930s are shown here reading from a script into a microphone, including legendary film actor Joan Crawford (*far right*).

The success of the *Orphan Annie* radio show demonstrated that Annie was a character who appealed to all ages, and a live performance based on the character's adventures could attract a sizable audience. It also set the precedent that scripts for live performance did not have to conform to Annie's experiences in the comic strip. The head writer, Frank Dahm, was allowed to create his own adventures for Annie.

Little Orphan Annie at the Movies

In 1932, Annie made her move from radio to the movies in a motion picture called *Little Orphan Annie*. The film was directed by John S. Robertson and featured a script written by Tom McNamara and Wanda Tuchock. Like the later musical, it was based on the comic strip by Harold Gray.

Mitzi Green, shown here, was a popular child star of the 1930s.

It starred twelve-year-old Mitzi Green as Annie. Green had already starred in several films made by Paramount Pictures, including *Tom Sawyer* (1930) and *Huckleberry Finn* (1931). Daddy Warbucks was played by Edgar Kennedy, who had worked in films by Mack Sennett (known for his Keystone Kops comedies), and by Charlie Chaplin. The film was made by RKO Pictures under the guidance of legendary producer David O. Selznick.

In the film, Annie is left alone while Daddy Warbucks is away on an extended trip. Annie rescues a boy named Mickey who is about to be taken to the orphanage. Eventually, both Mickey and Annie wind up in the orphanage. When a rich woman, Mrs. Stewart, expresses an interest in adopting a child, Annie deliberately draws her attention to Mickey, and Mrs. Stewart adopts him. The plot turns to farce as Annie attempts to visit Mickey at the Stewart house during a dinner party, and Sandy steals the main course, while Mrs. Stewart mistakes a stealthily escaping Annie for a ghost. After the plot is resolved, Mrs. Stewart throws a party for all the orphans from the orphanage. Annie finds that the Santa at the party is really Daddy Warbucks, and the film ends happily. The film was not a great success, but that did not stop Paramount from making its own attempt in 1938. The 1932 movie shared a Christmas setting with the 1977 musical, but its farcical tone had more in common with the 1982 movie version of *Annie* than with the Broadway play.

In 1938, Paramount Studios embarked on its own version of Annie. This film was also titled *Little Orphan Annie*. It was directed by Ben Holmes, and the screenplay was written by Samuel Ornitz, Budd Schulberg, and Endre Bohem. This time the film featured Ann Gillis, a child star under contract to Warner Brothers who the studio hoped would be another Shirley Temple—the most popular child star of the day. The main character is called Annie, never Little Orphan Annie, despite the film's title. In the film, Annie becomes friends with a boxing manager, "Pop" Corrigan, and introduces him to a promising prizefighter, Johnny Adams. She convinces the local people to foot the cost of Johnny's training, as an investment opportunity. He's so good that on the night he's supposed to have his big fight, the local gambling syndicate locks him in a gym. When it looks like Annie, Johnny, and the townspeople are doomed to lose their investment, a group of housewives comes to their rescue. The film, which lacks Daddy Warbucks, bore little resemblance to the comic strip beyond the fact that Annie was an orphan and a tough little girl. It made little impression on the public.

More Than a Comic Strip

This illustration shows Oliver from Dickens's *Oliver Twist*. Like Annie, he was an orphan.

In some ways, *Annie* owes as much to the novels of Charles Dickens as to Gray's comic strip. Lyricist and director Martin Charnin, who conceived the idea for the musical, is a big fan of Dickens, especially his portrayal of poor and orphaned children. In several of Dickens's works, an appealing child must use his or her resourcefulness to overcome great obstacles and, in some cases, achieve a happy ending. When Charnin read Gray's comic strips, Annie struck him as that kind of character. He felt that her story would be adaptable to the stage in much the same way as Dickens's stories (such as *Oliver Twist*) were. Charnin wanted the play *Annie* to have a Dickensian feel and not just be a musical version of a comic strip. (It should be kept in mind that the 1982 movie of *Annie* does not represent the original vision of the stage play, which was less slapstick and cartoony, and more touching.)

Annie fulfilled Charnin's view of the two ingredients necessary to make a musical. The first is a main character who has a mission or quest and is engaging and interesting enough to hold the audience's interest for two hours on stage. The second is a suitable setting—in this case New York City during the Great Depression.

The Story

The stage version of Annie used the characters in the comic strip, but not any of Gray's story lines. Instead, the creators of the play, Charnin and his collaborators, composer Charles Strouse and scriptwriter Thomas Meehan, decided to answer a question left unaddressed in the comic strip: How did Annie and billionaire businessman Oliver Warbucks meet?

The play is set in 1933, and Annie is an eleven-year-old foundling at the Municipal Girls' Orphanage. Annie defends a younger orphan from other girls and sings the song "Maybe," in which she fantasizes about what her parents are doing and expresses how she longs for them. Annie tries to escape in an effort to find her parents, but she is caught by the alcoholic Miss Hannigan, who runs the orphanage. Angry at being disturbed, Miss Hannigan forces all the girls to scrub the orphanage. As they work, they sing one of the show's two signature songs, "It's a Hard-Knock Life." When the laundry man arrives to collect the linens, Miss Hannigan flirts with him. While Miss Hannigan is occupied, Annie climbs into the laundry basket and escapes.

Having escaped, Annie meets a stray dog. She protects him from the dogcatcher by claiming he's hers. To comfort

Miss Hannigan, who manages the orphanage, punishes Annie and the girls for disturbing her.

him, she sings the other signature song from the show, "Tomorrow." She finds her way to a Hooverville, a community formed by people left homeless by the Great Depression. A policeman sent by Miss Hannigan to find Annie catches her and returns her to the orphanage.

Grace Farrell, Warbucks's assistant, arrives at the orphanage to invite an orphan to join Warbucks at his mansion for Christmas, for public relations purposes. She chooses Annie. Miss Hannigan is unhappy at Annie's good luck but is forced to agree.

At the Warbucks mansion, Oliver Warbucks is not delighted to be faced with an orphan, especially not a little girl. He asks Farrell to take her to a movie, but Farrell insists that he go as well. Warbucks and Annie have a good time together, but Annie still longs for her parents. Grace and the staff vow they will locate her parents, and Warbucks announces on the radio that he is offering $50,000 to the couple who can prove they are her parents. Miss Hannigan's brother, Rooster, and his girlfriend, Lily, show up at the orphanage with a plan to pose as Annie's parents to get the reward. They persuade Miss Hannigan to give them inside information on Annie in return for a share of the reward.

When Daddy Warbucks goes to Washington, DC, for a meeting with President Roosevelt, he takes Annie with him. When they return home, Warbucks admits to Annie that he's come to love her and wants to adopt her. They plan a Christmas party to which Annie invites Miss Hannigan and the orphans.

Rooster and Lily show up at the mansion, disguised as Mr. and Mrs. Mudge, to claim Annie as their daughter. Despite the evidence they bring, Warbucks doubts they are her real parents. He gets them to agree to let her stay one more day for the Christmas party. The next morning, President Roosevelt pays Warbucks a visit and reveals the identity of Annie's real parents, explaining that they died when she was a baby. When Rooster and Lily show up to pick up Annie—and the money—they are arrested by the Secret Service, along with Miss Hannigan. Everyone is pleased by Roosevelt's New Deal for the economy (a clear departure from Gray's views in the comic strip). They sing "A New Deal for Christmas" and "Tomorrow."

Gray probably would have disapproved of the scene. He disliked happy endings. It's true that Annie always won out over her enemies, but Gray frequently incorporated a twist at the end that left Annie in another tough spot. Audiences, however, love the show's finale.

Chapter 2

The Road to Broadway

The road to Broadway was long and hard for the creators of *Annie*. It is a struggle under any circumstances to get a play to Broadway, but the task is doubly difficult when dealing with a play based on a comic strip.

Martin Charnin wrote the lyrics for the songs in *Annie* and directed the show; the music for the songs was composed by Charles Strouse. It was Charnin who first conceived the idea of creating a musical based on the *Little Orphan Annie* comic strip at Christmas time in 1971. While searching for a Christmas gift in the Doubleday bookstore on Fifty-Seventh Street in New York, he came across a book titled *Arf! The Life and Hard Times of Little Orphan Annie*. The book included ten years' worth of Harold Gray's *Little*

Opposite: Annie's composer, Charles Strouse, and lyricist, Martin Charnin

Orphan Annie comic strip. Although he'd bought the book as a gift, he spent the night reading it. The next day, he had his lawyer investigate whether the rights were available to make a play based on the strip.

Little Orphan Annie was one of the earliest comic strips to feature a continuing story rather than the one-off comic gags that were usual for strips of the time. The fact that she had a story and that it grew from week to week and year to year drew readers into her life and made her a more engaging character. In a 2016 interview with Roger Catlin in the *Washington Post*, Charnin said:

> I loved the way [the comic strip] was drawn. I thought Harold Gray was a wonderful cartoonist … *Annie* had long stories that lasted two or three months, and he would connect one adventure to the next adventure that he came up with.

According to Charnin in the *Washington Post* interview, "When you're writing musicals you look for them wherever you can find them—in films, in short stories, in a painting, in a bubble-gum wrapper, if it came to that."

Charnin picked up on the fact that nowhere in the comic did Gray explain how Annie and Daddy Warbucks came to meet. This gave him the chance to create a story that was different from anything in the comic. Charnin and his collaborators, Thomas Meehan and Charles Strouse, wanted to create a musical set in the 1930s during the Great Depression because, as Charnin has put it:

[It's] lovely and rewarding to remind cynics of the world that every now and again, it looks pretty crummy out there, and somebody is saying, "The sun will come out tomorrow."

Their focus when they started constructing the play was that "there is a better day around the corner." In 1970, Charnin paid the *Chicago Tribune* $7,500 for the rights to adapt the *Little Orphan Annie* comic strip. He spent all the money he had renewing the options for seven years, until he was able to open the musical *Annie* on Broadway.

Early Decision

The book, or script, for the show was written by Meehan, who died August 22, 2017, at the age of eighty-eight. He was born in 1929 in Ossining, New York. When he was still a child, he decided he wanted to be a writer of short stories or novels. He was embarrassed to admit that ambition, however, so he told people he planned to be a lawyer. In the 1940s, as teens, he and his brother would manage to collect enough money to pay for the cheapest seats, then take the bus to New York City to watch Broadway shows, seeing such musicals as Rodgers and Hammerstein's *Oklahoma!*

Meehan graduated from Hamilton College in Clinton, New York. At age twenty-four, he moved to New York City and obtained a job writing for the *New Yorker* magazine, where he stayed for ten years. He didn't start working in the theater until after he was forty, when Charnin got him to agree to write the book for *Annie*.

Annie's scriptwriter, Thomas Meehan, wanted to write for Broadway from the time he was a boy.

Meehan went on to a successful career writing books for other musicals such as *Hairspray* and screenplays for films, including Mel Brooks's *Spaceballs*. Meehan wanted his musicals to have happy endings so the audience would leave the theater with smiles on their faces. His goal was to give people a good time. Meehan won three Tony awards for musicals: for *Annie* in 1977, for *The Producers* in 2001, and as coauthor with Mark O'Donnell for *Hairspray* in 2003.

Charnin met Meehan in 1972, when Charnin was directing a television special that included a sketch based on a piece Meehan had written for the *New Yorker*. Charnin told Meehan that with his writing style, he could do the book for a musical, and he gave Meehan that chance when he invited him to work on *Annie*. Meehan didn't embrace the project with unbridled enthusiasm, however. When Charnin first broached the idea of creating a musical based on the comic strip, Meehan hated it. Charnin convinced him the play wouldn't be performed as if it were a comic; the characters would play it as if they were real people.

Having won Meehan over, Charnin invited Strouse to meet with him and Meehan. When Charnin pitched Strouse the idea of a musical based on *Little Orphan Annie*, Strouse also hated the idea. Other attempts had been made to mount Broadway shows based on comics, such as *Superman*, and they had been flops. Again Charnin explained that, instead of making the musical "cartoony," they would play it straight, making Annie an appealing, lost, little girl. Once Charnin convinced Strouse to join the project, Meehan came up with an outline for the play. He wanted one or, at most, two characters that the audience would meet at the beginning of the play. The main character would face a dilemma and want something very much. The audience would follow her story until she finally got what she wanted. Meehan has said that he only loosely based his Annie on the comic strip character. Instead, he tried to make the story about a child's quest for her missing parents.

Setting Suggested

When Charnin first discussed the concept for the musical with Meehan, Meehan suggested setting the story in the two weeks before Christmas in 1933. Having decided to tell the story as if the characters were real, they dropped two supporting characters from the comic strip—Daddy's Warbucks's Indian assistant, Punjab, who had mystical powers, and Punjab's sidekick, the Asp.

The three collaborators were all New Yorkers, and they all agreed that they wanted to set the play in New York City. In the 1970s, when they created the play, New York was undergoing a financial crisis. Parts of the city were run down, and crime was rampant. The country was politically divided, and protests were common over the Vietnam War and racial issues. President Richard M. Nixon and his administration were corrupt and engaged in illegal activity that eventually led to Nixon's impeachment and resignation. They took Meehan's suggestion to set the play in 1933, in the midst of the Great Depression—another period characterized by unrest and despair. Meehan saw Annie as representing courage, decency, resilience, optimism, and hope in an era of pessimism and hard times.

According to Charnin, two key elements form the focus of the play. First, there is the fact that Annie is a foundling. Technically, she is not an orphan, because she was left on the steps of the orphanage but might have living parents somewhere. The search for Annie's parents is the second key element of the story of Warbucks meeting her, coming to love her, and adopting her.

In 1972, Meehan began working on the book for the play, while Charnin and Strouse worked out the score. They did not have a producer for the show. One of the roles of the producer is to obtain funding for the production, usually by lining up investors, who put up money in return for a share of the profits if the show is successful. Because there was no producer, the three collaborators did not have money to pay themselves a salary. Thus, they had to continue to make a living in other ways while working on the book and score. They met every few weeks. The show took sixteen months to complete.

According to Meehan, there is a difference between writing a book for a musical and writing a nonmusical play. In a musical, the written part of each scene is only two to three pages long. The concept is to build up to an emotional point that is too strong for words and then transition to a song.

Today, *Annie* is widely seen as a musical for young people, especially teenaged and preteen girls, but the play's creators conceived it as a play for adults. They didn't think of it as a family show or a children's show for children, but as a musical for adults. Indeed, when it first opened on Broadway, the audience consisted primarily of adults. About six weeks into the play's run, however, many of the adults who had been to see it came back with their children.

The Search for a Producer

Once the score and book were completed, Charnin, Meehan, and Strouse set about trying to find a producer. Initially, Charnin pitched the show to numerous New York producers, hoping to get the work produced on Broadway. To get producers to put on a show, one auditions it for them,

MARTIN CHARNIN

Martin Charnin was born in New York City in 1934. A talented painter, he attended the High School of Music and Art in New York City. After graduating, he attended Cooper Union in New York, from which he received a bachelor of fine arts degree. He began acting when he worked with a theater group at a small resort in the Adirondack Mountains. Although he spent as much time waiting tables as acting, he was hooked. He played Big Deal, a member of the Jets, in the musical *West Side Story* on Broadway and subsequently on tour. Charnin wrote music and lyrics for a number of Off-Broadway plays and revues. He then turned to writing and directing nightclub acts for performers such as Dionne Warwick, José Ferrer, and Leslie Uggams.

In 1963, he wrote the lyrics for a Broadway musical for the first time. The show was *Hot Spot*, and the music was written by Mary Rodgers. He wrote the lyrics for several more musicals, including *Two by Two* in 1970. For this production, he worked with Richard Rodgers, who did the music. Rodgers was well known for a series of musicals he had written with Oscar Hammerstein. The play starred Danny Kaye and lasted for ten months on Broadway.

Charnin turned his attention to television in the early 1970s, writing, producing, and directing television variety specials. He won Emmy Awards for *Annie; The Women in the Life of a Man*, which starred Anne Bancroft; and *'S Wonderful, 'S Marvelous, 'S Gershwin*, which starred Jack Lemmon, Fred Astaire, and Ethel Merman, among others.

He began his Broadway directing career in 1973, designing and directing *Nash at Nine*, a revue based on the works of Ogden Nash. He subsequently directed several other revues, including *The National Lampoon Show* in 1975, which starred John Belushi, Gilda Radner, Bill Murray, and various other performers from *Saturday Night Live*.

Martin Charnin (*far right*) accepts an Emmy Award early in his career.

In 1977, he scored his biggest hit when he wrote the lyrics for and directed *Annie*, which became one of the twenty-five longest-running musicals on Broadway. He subsequently directed the five US national touring companies of *Annie* and three productions in the West End in London, Britain's equivalent of Broadway.

In 1979, he wrote the lyrics for *I Remember Mama*, for which Richard Rodgers did the music. He directed, wrote the lyrics for, and cowrote the book for *The First* (1981), a musical about Jackie Robinson and the integration of baseball. Throughout the 1980s, he directed Broadway and Off-Broadway plays.

In the 1990s, he directed numerous US and international productions of *Annie*, including in Australia and Amsterdam. Charnin is artistic director of *Showtunes!*, in Seattle, Washington, which revives forgotten musicals.

or performs an abbreviated version of it, hoping a producer will like it enough to back it. The first producer they tried, in 1973, was James Nederlander. He was enthusiastic about the play after the audition and asked to see the script. However, Nederlander was involved in other projects and couldn't do the play in the timeframe Charnin, Meehan, and Strouse were looking for. They wanted to get the play mounted immediately, if possible, and they were convinced that if a producer of Nederlander's caliber found it interesting, so would others. Two and a half years later, they were still trying to find a producer.

According to Charnin in his book *Annie: A Theatre Memoir*, the problem was that, although producers liked the score, they had trouble visualizing the play as a real story of a girl searching for her parents. Instead, they imagined the story would be camp or cartoony. Also, the show's creators wanted to cast a real child as the star, rather than hire an actress with name recognition and try to make her look like a youngster. Producers were afraid that a play without a big-name star would lack audience draw. To make the situation more difficult, Charnin wanted to direct the show himself.

Failing to find anyone in New York willing to produce *Annie*, Charnin thought of the Goodspeed Opera House in East Haddam, Connecticut, which put on musicals. Each season it typically produced two revivals of musicals and one original show. At first, the executive director of Goodspeed, Michael Price, wasn't any more enthusiastic than the New York producers had been. But shortly after rejecting the show, he found that he kept humming the show's songs.

He contacted Charnin and told him he had changed his mind and would produce the show on the main stage at Goodspeed. Price was adamant, however, about not having Charnin direct the show, instead giving him the choice of the theater's resident director or an outside one. Desperate to get the show produced, Charnin made the painful decision to give up the directing role. *Annie*'s creators insisted that, if Charnin was not going to direct, they should have approval of the director who took over. Price recommended three people. Charnin, Meehan, and Strouse talked with them all, discussing their vision for the show. All three directors had trouble with the idea of *Annie* as a reality-based show rather than one performed with an element of tongue in cheek. Charnin and his collaborators decided that none of the directors suggested by Price was suitable. Reluctantly, Price agreed to let Charnin direct the show.

Charnin, Meehan, and Strouse returned to New York to cast *Annie*. They auditioned more than six hundred people over three weeks. They chose fifteen actors who performed in the Goodspeed production and went with the show to Broadway. Casting the character of Annie was especially difficult. There was no lack of little girls from six to thirteen to choose from, but most of them had already been trained by the entertainment industry to be stylish and professional. That was not what Charnin was looking for. He wanted a natural little girl, whom he could shape into his ideal version of Annie. He and his collaborators were also looking for little girls of specific types to make a group of orphans, each of whom would have a distinct personality. The first orphan they cast was Andrea McArdle. She combined a strong work ethic and sense of humor with a street-smart attitude. They chose Kristen Vigard, a thirteen-year-old girl with naturally red hair, to play the part of Annie. Having assembled a group of six child actors, the collaborators turned their attention to "the dog."

PHONY BALONEY

Like the human actors, Sandy had to perform the same movements each night. For a scene in which Sandy needs to cross the stage, Charnin had an actor on stage drop a piece of bologna each night to draw Sandy across the stage.

In the Nick of Time

Finding a dog to play Annie's companion, Sandy, was not easy. They failed to find a suitable dog through the New York casting agency, so they embarked on a search of dog pounds, animal shelters, and even individual dog owners. Finally, eighteen-year-old William Berloni, one of the technicians at Goodspeed, found "Sandy" at the dog pound in Newington, Connecticut. It took Charnin one look to realize that Berloni had found the perfect dog. That was good news for the nine-month-old pup, since he was one day away from being put to sleep. The cost for the dog was eight dollars. There was one difficulty with Sandy, however. It became apparent that he had been abused at some point

Pound dog "Sandy" became an endearing and popular star with fans of his own.

by someone who had dressed in dark clothing, as the dog reacted badly to people dressed in dark blue. Since he had two scenes with uniformed policemen, he had to be gently retrained to trust them. (According to Martin Charnin in *Annie: A Theatre Memoir*, Thomas Meehan wanted to bill Sandy in the cast list as "last but not leashed.")

Charnin, as director, had only sixteen weeks to design and rehearse the production at the Goodspeed. This was a daunting task. He had a group of actors who had never worked with him or each other, and he had to meld them into a team. He had to block the show (establish the location and movements of the actors). He had imagined the blocking for the show in his head, but faced with the size and shape of the stage at the Goodspeed, he had to start the process anew. The stage was only 23 feet (7 meters) deep. There was no wing space in which to put stage pieces, and there were fourteen set changes in the show. The stage wasn't the only thing that was small. East Haddam itself was a small town, and something of a culture shock for Charnin, the New Yorker. He took up residence in a renovated apple barn, walking a mile to the theater each day. The actors were put up in boarding houses. Time was short, so rehearsals took place eight hours a day. According to Charnin in *Annie: A Theatre Memoir*, "We rehearsed at the theatre, in the public library, on the lawn, at every meal at the restaurant—morning, noon, and night—until August 9, the night of the dress rehearsal."

Unfortunately, the creators' trials weren't over. On the night of the dress rehearsal, a large hurricane hit the East Coast. It knocked out electric power in New York and Connecticut, including East Haddam. A local audience had been invited to attend the dress rehearsal, a process that allows the actors and director to get a feel for how an audience will react. However, after forty minutes, the audience had left. Not only couldn't they see, but the air conditioning wasn't working. The cast and crew struggled to rehearse the entire play, but after working from 9 p.m. until 2 a.m., they gave up without getting all the way through. After everyone else had left, Charnin stayed up with the stage manager and crew, working until 5 a.m. Had the power remained off, the opening could have been postponed, but the electricity came back on at 11 a.m. This left them with no choice but to go on with the show.

Making Changes

Annie premiered on August 10, 1976. The show was long—three and a half hours—and some of the scene changes took way too long. However, the Goodspeed's audience, used to opening night issues, was tolerant, and its response to the show was positive. Seeing how long the show ran, Charnin knew that cuts needed to be made to bring it down to a reasonable running time.

The theater critics came on the fourth day of the show. Approximately thirty-five critics came from towns around Connecticut. According to Martin Charnin, about twenty wrote positive reviews, five hated the show, and ten were somewhere in between. Changes needed to be made, and to decide which issues had to be dealt with, the show's creators focused on the reviews in the middle—those that provided constructive criticism rather than wild enthusiasm or loathing.

One problem was the actress playing Annie, Kristen Vigard. She was pretty, appealing, and talented, but she lacked the feistiness that was central to Annie's character. After the first week of performances, it was obvious to Charnin and his collaborators that they would need to replace her. Charnin hated the idea of firing a child, but if he wanted the play to succeed, he had to do it. To replace

Vigard in the role, Charnin chose Andrea McArdle, who played Pepper, the toughest of the orphans. With McArdle playing a streetwise Annie, the play came together, sparking a much stronger reaction in audiences. Word of mouth spread interest in the play, and Price extended the planned ten-week run of the show by another three weeks.

Meanwhile, Charnin, Meehan, and Strouse worked continuously, fixing the play's flaws. They rewrote scenes, cut some songs, and rearranged others. They added the song "Maybe," in which Annie speculates about the kind of people her parents are and hopes they'll realize their mistake in leaving her. That song highlighted the central theme for the play by providing a heightened sense of reality to the orphans' condition and emphasizing that Annie was longing for her real mother and father.

Charnin, Meehan, and Strouse still hoped to take the show to Broadway, but they had a hard time getting producers from New York to drive to an unknown theater in Connecticut. In an interview, Charnin said, "To them, it was Juneau, Alaska. Nobody came." The New York producers didn't get the concept, thinking the show was a cartoon or satire, according to Charnin. To understand what it was like, producers had to see it, and to see it they would have to drive to Connecticut.

On August 27, *New York Times* theater critic Walter Kerr came to see the show. Kerr was a powerful force in defining the future of a play. The show's creators hoped for a positive review that would help them get the show to Broadway, but Kerr gave them a bad review. Before going to

Andrea McArdle, the actress who played Annie in Connecticut and on Broadway, poses in character with Sandy and Daddy Warbucks.

CHARLES STROUSE

Charles Strouse was born in New York City in 1928. When he was ten, he began taking piano lessons, and at fifteen, he enrolled in the University of Rochester Eastman School of Music, graduating in 1947. He won two scholarships to Tanglewood, a renowned music center in the Berkshire Mountains of western Massachusetts. There, he studied under legendary American composer Aaron Copland. Strouse's early music-related jobs included scoring and composing music for Twentieth Century Fox newsreels and writing dance music.

While attending a party in 1949, he met lyricist Lee Adams at a party, and the duo began writing songs for various revues and for performers such as Carol Burnett. In 1958, Strouse and Adams auditioned to be the writing team for *Bye Bye Birdie*, a musical about American teenagers. After three rounds of auditions, they won the job. The show premiered on Broadway in 1960 and was a hit. It won six Tony Awards, including Best Musical, beating such great musicals as *Camelot* and *The Unsinkable Molly Brown*.

Strouse has composed scores for more than thirty stage musicals, fourteen of which appeared on Broadway, as well as scores for five Hollywood films. He wrote the theme song "Those Were the Days" for the TV series *All in the Family*. Four of Strouse's Broadway musicals were subsequently produced on television: *Applause* in 1973, *It's a Bird … It's a Plane … It's Superman* in 1975, *Bye Bye Birdie* in 1995, and *Annie*, which appeared on *The Wonderful World of Disney* on ABC in 1999. The Disney production of *Annie* still holds the position of the highest-rated television musical ever, according to television rating company Nielsen. The show won Strouse two Emmys and a Peabody Award, an award established by businessman George Foster Peabody to "honor the most powerful, enlightening, and invigorating stories in television, radio [and now online media]." Along with Strouse's work in theater, film, and television, his credits also include chamber and orchestral works and an opera, *Nightingale,* based on a Hans Christian Andersen story.

Charles Strouse at the time that *Annie* became a hit, with a poster advertising the Toronto tour

Besides the movie version of *Annie*, Strouse wrote the film scores for the movies *Bonnie & Clyde* (which won him a Grammy nomination), *There Was a Crooked Man*, *The Night They Raided Minsky's*, *Just Tell Me What You Want*, and *All Dogs Go to Heaven*. Strouse won Tony Awards for *Bye Bye Birdie*; *Applause*, a musical adaptation of the movie *All About Eve*; and *Annie*. He is a member of the Songwriters Hall of Fame.

East Haddam, Charnin had held discussions with potential producers Irwin Meyer and Stephen R. Friedman. They were interested in making the show their first Broadway production. However, Kerr's negative review, which implied that the show wouldn't make it in New York, made them question the viability of the play.

Then, in the last week of the Goodspeed run, Lewis Allen, a friend of Charles Strouse, came to see the show. Allen and Strouse had worked together on a play in London. Allen asked his partner, director Mike Nichols, to come up to see the production. In the show's last weekend, Nichols came. He originally had the same reservations about a show based on *Little Orphan Annie* that Meehan and Strouse had had when Charnin first suggested the idea to them. However, like Lewis, when Nichols saw the show, he loved it. Nonetheless, Nichols insisted he wasn't a producer. Charnin, Meehan, and Strouse thought their hopes of taking the show to Broadway were doomed. Then Nichols changed his mind. The morning after seeing the play, he called Charnin and said that he and Allen had discussed it on the drive back to New York and had decided to produce it on Broadway with Meyer and Friedman. Charnin says, "It was unbelievable. It was like winning the Grand Prix. Stunning. It was the rope thrown to you just as you're about to go down for the third time."

When the show closed in Connecticut, Charnin, Meehan, and Strouse returned to New York and set about working with the producers to raise the money to mount the musical on Broadway. A lot of money had to be raised. According to Martin Charnin in *Annie: A*

American film and
theater director
Mike Nichols

Theatre Memoir, the show required: "20 musicians, 16
sets, 185 costumes ... Fees and salaries had to be added
for stagehands, electricians, sound personnel, press agents,
general managers, advertising personnel." The show that
was mounted in East Haddam for $70,000 would ultimately
cost one million dollars to produce on Broadway. The
group formed a limited partnership for investors. Based on
an estimated budget of $650,000, they sold shares in the
partnership for $1,500 each. Ultimately, about thirty people
invested in the show.

Chapter 3

Broadway

*A*nnie opened at the Alvin Theatre (now the Neil Simon Theatre) on Broadway on April 21, 1977. It was directed by Martin Charnin and choreographed by Peter Gennaro. The cast included Andrea McArdle as Annie, Reid Shelton as Daddy Warbucks, Dorothy Loudon as Miss Hannigan, and Sandy Faison as Grace Farrell. The play was nominated for ten Tony Awards, given for excellence in Broadway theater, and won seven of them. (The maximum it could have won was nine since both Andrea McArdle and Dorothy Loudon were nominated for Best Actress.) The show set the record for longest-running show at the Alvin Theatre. That record was not surpassed until *Hairspray!* in 2009.

When the show moved to Broadway, the creators took the opportunity to recast the role of Miss Hannigan. Miss Hannigan was intended to be mean because she's stuck in the job of running the orphanage—the only job she could get—and the girls were more than she could cope with.

Opposite: This scene from the original Broadway production of *Annie* shows Annie with Daddy Warbucks and his servants, who support her.

However, the show's creators also wanted her to be funny. They felt that the actress who played her in Connecticut, Maggie Task, had done a good job of portraying her meanness but wasn't very funny. Actress Dorothy Loudon took over the role and ended up winning a Tony Award as well as receiving rave reviews for her performance.

Dorothy Loudon brought both sternness and humor to the role of Miss Hannigan.

Broadway Run:
April 21, 1977–
January 2, 1983

Venue:
Alvin Theatre

**Number of
Performances:** 2,377

FACTS ABOUT *ANNIE*

1977 Tony Awards
Best Musical
Best Book for a Musical: Thomas Meehan
Best Original Score: Martin Charnin and Charles Strouse
Best Leading Actress in a Musical: Dorothy Loudon (Miss Hannigan;
Andrea McArdle was also nominated for playing Annie)
Best Scenic Design: David Mitchell
Best Choreography: Peter Gennaro
Best Costume Design: Theoni V. Aldredge
Martin Charnin was nominated for Best Director, but didn't win.

New York Drama Desk Awards
Outstanding Musical
Outstanding Book of a Musical: Thomas Meehan
Outstanding Featured Actress in a Musical: Dorothy Loudon
Outstanding Director of a Musical: Martin Charnin
Outstanding Choreography: Peter Gennaro
Outstanding Lyrics: Martin Charnin
Outstanding Costume Design: Theoni V. Aldredge

Other Awards
New York Drama Critics Award: Best Musical 1976–1977
1978 Grammy Award: Best Cast Album

Annie was a large musical that was very technically complicated and difficult to produce. The show required twenty-three actors plus three "swing" actors who didn't have a role but filled in as needed. Some of the actors in minor roles were also understudies for the major actors. If a major actor became ill, the understudy would take his or her place, and one of the swing actors would take the minor role. There was also an understudy for Sandy the dog, a dog named Arf. The crew included thirty-three carpenters, electricians, flymen (stagehands who lower scenery to the stage from above), sliders (stagehands who push scenery on and pull it off), and a soundman. Running the show required four stage managers: supervisory production stage manager Janet Beroza; a stage manager who actually ran the show, giving the cues to the crew; and two assistant stage managers. There was a wardrobe supervisor with a team of twelve dressers. They were responsible for helping the actors change costumes, and for sorting, cleaning, and fixing costumes after the performance, so they would be ready for the next performance. An orchestra played the music for the production numbers. It consisted of musical director Peter Howard, an assistant musical director, and eighteen musicians.

New costumes, sets, and orchestration were created for the show's Broadway debut. Charnin, Meehan, and Strouse were still rewriting the play as well. For example, after trying several times to rewrite a scene that took place in a low-end restaurant, they replaced it altogether with a new scene set in a Hooverville, a location where people who were left homeless by the Great Depression built temporary shelters. The name comes from Herbert Hoover, who was the president of the United States when the Great Depression started. In the process of altering the scene, the show's creators replaced the song "We Got Annie," with "We'd Like to Thank You, Herbert Hoover." Martin Charnin estimates that about 25 percent of *Annie* changed between the first draft and its opening on Broadway. He notes that sometimes a musical number just doesn't work, and often the best approach is to throw it out and start from scratch.

Grand Vision

One thing that the show's creators were determined to do was create a high-production-value show—one with elaborate sets. In the 1970s, it was common for plays to use minimal sets and rely on the audience to fill in the setting with their imagination. Charnin, Meehan, and Strouse wanted to create elaborate sets and costumes that would impress the audience. They hired David Mitchell to design the sets and Theoni Aldredge to design the costumes. Mitchell had designed sets for the New York City Ballet and the New York City Opera. He was nominated for a Tony award for his *Annie* sets. Theoni Aldredge had designed costumes for musicals such as *Hair!* and *A Chorus Line* as well as the New York Shakespeare Company. She had won an Oscar for her work on the movie *The Great Gatsby*.

While the play was being set up in New York, Bill Berloni, the technician who had discovered Sandy, took him to a dog-training school in New York. He was taught the tricks he would do on stage. Sandy had six tricks: he had

FINANCING THE SHOW

The set for *Annie* was complex. It incorporated a deck and two treadmills that moved the set. Quite a number of set pieces had to be lowered from above. Mitchell did extensive research for the sets at the New York Public Library, the Bettman Archives, and other sources that had pictures of New York in the 1930s. All the buildings in the show represented actual locations in 1930s New York. The set ended up costing $185,000 (the equivalent of about $729,000 in 2017). William Grimes stated in his *New York Times* obituary of Mitchell:

> His sets for *Annie*, contrasting the grim reality of New York during the Depression with the opulence of the Daddy Warbucks mansion, played a major role in the show's success.

Harking back to the comic strip, the show's creators wanted to get the effect of Harold Gray's shading onto the buildings in the set. Lighting designer Judy Rasmuson was able to create a lighting plan that echoed Gray's style of contrasting light and dark areas. Costumes for the show were expensive too, because they were all being created from scratch.

All these expenses exceeded the show's original budget. In order to raise more money, Charnin, Meehan, and Strouse started to hold weekly auditions for potential backers. They were aided in raising money by Sam Cohn, the agent from International Creative Management who represented the producers Mike Nichols and Lewis Allen. Cohn assisted them with dealmaking and negotiations. The play was due to start rehearsals in December, but Andrea McArdle, who was playing Annie, came down with mononucleosis, and Charnin, Meehan, and Strouse were still in the midst of fundraising, so rehearsals didn't start until January.

A big stage show requires big dance numbers. To replace the simple dance numbers used in the Connecticut production, Peter Gennaro, the choreographer of *West Side Story,* was hired to create new ones. Peter Howard, who had been musical director for such famous Broadway shows as *Hello, Dolly!* and *Mame*, was hired as musical director.

Meyer and Friedman had collected $250,000 from their investors, and Nichols and Allen had collected $250,000 from theirs. However, the week before rehearsals were scheduled to start, the company was still $300,000 short of meeting its budget. Producer Roger Stevens of the Kennedy Center and producer Jimmy Nederlander supplied the money to make up the shortfall, allowing the show to go on.

IT'S A DOG'S LIFE

Sandy, the dog found at the Connecticut Humane Society, missed only fourteen of the 2,377 performances of *Annie*'s original Broadway run. He was absent from the stage only because he was taken to Las Vegas for an appearance with Liberace and the original Annie, Andrea McArdle. Sandy died in his sleep in August 1990 at the age of sixteen, according to his owner, Bill Berloni.

to be pushed onstage; to stand on the mark where Annie meets him; to roll over when she asks if he's been hurt; to lie on his back while the actors talk about him; to jump up and put his paws on Annie's shoulders when she calls him; and to walk across an empty stage supposedly looking for Annie. The last trick was the most difficult. In his book *Annie: A Theatre Memoir*, Martin Charnin says Sandy never misbehaved on stage. He notes:

> Sometimes he misses his cue because his attention span is short, but the one crucial trick, that important one of walking across, sitting down and slowly doing a Jack Benny take—he does that perfectly every time.

Rehearsals were held at the Broadway Arts Studios over five weeks. Charnin was finally able to concentrate on the creative aspects of the play. He spent four hours of every day just working with the children.

Annie sings to Sandy to cheer him up. McArdle became very attached to Sandy during the show.

Press agent David Powers was hired to publicize the show. He succeeded in getting the press interested. And the media members weren't the only people curious about the show. While the play was still in rehearsal, the social secretary for the White House, Gretchen Poston, showed up at the studio. She was a friend of Roger Stevens of the Kennedy Center in Washington, DC, and had heard about the show. Every year, the president of the United States hosts a dinner for all the state governors, as well as members of the Supreme Court and the Cabinet and their spouses. The president at the time was Jimmy Carter, and he had sent Poston to audition the show as possible entertainment for the Governors' Dinner. After watching various numbers from the show, Poston asked for a twenty-five minute performance at the dinner.

Washington Tryout

Before the play opened on Broadway, it had an out-of-town trial run at the Kennedy Center. The purpose of an out-of-town tryout is to test whether a play works and to fix any problems before moving to Broadway. If the play is unpopular with audiences, it may never get to Broadway at all. The Washington performances were a nervous time for the show's creators. The Eisenhower Theater at the Kennedy Center seated 1,100 people. Without a big-name star to draw an audience, the advance ticket sales were small. In order for the show to continue on to Broadway, it would need a good audience response in Washington—and that meant getting good reviews.

The entrance to the Eisenhower Theatre at the Kennedy Center in Washington, DC, where the Broadway version of *Annie* was tried out

On February 24, the show headed to Washington. There were a number of issues that had to be dealt with when the production was moved from the Goodspeed to the Kennedy Center. For one thing, the stage at the Eisenhower was 41 feet (12.5 meters) wide, twice the size of the one at the Goodspeed. Once the company arrived, the blocking had to be adjusted to fit the stage, and sets, costume, makeup, and orchestration had to be finalized. To make matters more complicated, there was the upcoming Governors' Dinner performance on March 1 to prepare for—and March 1 was the night of the play's first preview performance as well. In order to make both commitments, the preview was scheduled to start half an hour earlier than planned, and the performance at the White House half an hour later than originally planned, to allow the cast and crew to get from one destination to the other.

At 10 o'clock in the morning, the troupe performed a rehearsal of the twenty-five-minute condensed version of the play in the East Room of the White House. The press was allowed to take photographs during the run-through because they would not be allowed to do so at the Governors' Dinner. When the rehearsal was completed, the troupe boarded a chartered bus and returned to the Kennedy Center, where they rehearsed the preview performance. That evening they performed the revised version of the play in front of an audience for the first time. Much to everyone's relief, the audience's response was positive, and they gave the cast a standing ovation. The minute the curtain call was over, the troupe boarded the chartered bus and headed back to the White House. The children were given milk and cookies, and the troupe prepped for their performance. In the East Room, the president introduced the performance, and the show began. Music was provided by two pianos played by Peter Gennaro and Charles Strouse. The troupe received another standing ovation, this time led by the president of the United States. Gretchen Poston had incorporated the invitation to the dinner and the menu into a copy of the show's poster as a souvenir for the guests and the members of the troupe.

Although they were thrilled by the reaction to the two performances on March 1, Charnin, Meehan, and Strouse had no time to rest. The preview had revealed a number of issues that needed to be addressed before the play opened for its regular performances. Some scenes needed trimming, and there were technical problems with the enormous set that had to be attended to. They and the crew worked on the problems throughout the next week. Word-of-mouth recommendations spread from the preview audiences, and ticket sales began to pick up. By the time the show opened on Saturday, March 5, the house was full. The show garnered nine rave reviews from critics. The good reviews were magic. On Monday, March 7, the entire run of the show sold out. The press ran publicity items and interviews with members of the cast and the show's creators. Charnin wasn't lulled into a sense of security by the positive reaction in Washington, however. In the past, shows that had done well in Washington tryouts had been known to fail on Broadway.

Broadway

The Washington show closed in April, and the troupe headed back to New York—this time to the Alvin Theatre. For Charnin, it was something of a homecoming, because this was the theater in which he had played his first Broadway role as an actor, in *West Side Story*. Much of the same stage crew was still there and remembered him. The company had four days to set up before the first of eighteen previews prior to the show's official opening. Yet again, the show had to be adjusted to fit the new theater, which had a different stage, acoustics, and backstage space. There were constant meetings between Charnin, Meehan, Strouse, Gennaro, and Peter Howard. Now that they were in New York, they also needed to address the advertising for the show. Ads had to be designed for radio, TV, and newspapers. In addition, press publicity was important for drawing an audience, and that meant taking time away from the theater to do interviews with magazines and newspapers. Interviews appeared in *Vogue*, the *Village Voice*, *Newsweek*, *People*, and *New York* magazine. The well-known artist Al Hirschfeld drew a huge caricature of the cast, which ran in the *New York Times*.

Charnin was concerned that having all the New York critics in the house for opening night would put too much pressure on the cast. He asked the producers to arrange for critics to be allowed to attend one of three performances: the previews on Wednesday afternoon and Wednesday evening, and opening night on Thursday. According to Charnin in *Annie: A Theatre Memoir*, for the opening night, producer

AGING OUT

One of the problems related to *Annie* is that the actresses grow out of the part. As a young actress grows and matures, she looks inappropriate as an eleven-year-old. A number of times over the years, the actress playing Annie had to be replaced, including at one point by a young Sarah Jessica Parker of *Sex in the City* fame.

Mike Nichols let the cast and crew have as many tickets as they wanted for friends and family, but made the stipulation that those invited must not have seen the play before. This meant that their reactions would be fresh and genuine.

In *Annie: A Theatre Memoir*, Martin Charnin reveals that on opening night on Broadway, he gave everyone involved in the production a gift: the cast, crew, and orchestra received little, custom-made, silver Annies. He gave Charles Strouse a blow-up of a panel of the *Little Orphan Annie* comic strip, altered to include a list of all the songs that had been cut from the show since its inception. Tom Meehan got a plaque that said "The following characters have given their lives in the service of Thomas E. Meehan," followed by little brass plates containing the names of characters that had been cut from the musical during its development.

After the show, the producers threw an opening night party at Gallagher's Restaurant. At 11 p.m., Charnin, Meehan, and Strouse heard the television reviews and read the first ones in the newspapers. They were overwhelmingly positive. There were a few reviewers who didn't like the show, but it was clear the play was going to be a hit.

Putting on the Show

Putting on *Annie* required a production staff of ninety-six people. The preparation for the show began each night an hour before the show was due to start. The prop crew had to remove the set from the finale the night before, collect all the pieces of the set from where they had been left backstage when sets were changed, and gather all the props and put them in their proper places for the first scene. Meanwhile, the sound technician checked the speaker system, and the electricians checked for burned-out bulbs or gels (the colored film that covers some lights) and made sure the wiring was OK. The production stage manager, Janet Beroza, would go through a preset checklist to make sure everything was ready for the start of the play. All of the cast except for the actor playing Franklin Roosevelt, who doesn't appear until the second act, were required to be in the theater a half-hour before show time. By 7:30 p.m., the entire crew of stagehands was present, and the production manager rehearsed the actors' understudies on the set. This can only be done when stagehands are present because if a scene needs an element of the set to be rearranged, union rules require this to be done by stagehands.

The stage manager for the original production was Jack Timmers, and he controlled the crew and all the backstage activities. He had a standing desk on one side of

Members of the lighting crew adjust the lights for a performance of *Annie*.

the backstage area to hold the "prompt book," a copy of the script with all the cues for sound, lights, and the winch that moved the large pieces of the set. Timmers wore a headset through which he could talk to the crew during the show. He used a row of switches on the wall behind his desk to turn on lights that cued the flymen (who operated the ropes that swung scenery up), the light and soundboard operators, and the winch operators. During each performance, a television camera was used to shoot what was happening onstage so that Timmers would have a view of the complete stage while calling the cues for the technical crew. Today, a video camera and monitor are often used for the same purpose.

Fifteen minutes before curtain, the production stage manager and dance captain gave notes to the performers based on the previous evening's performance. By this point, the actors were costumed and made up and ready to go. Two minutes before the show was due to start, one of Timmers's assistant stage managers called, "Places for Act I." Timmers was in contact by headphone with the house manager, who let him know when the audience was all seated. Once he got the go-ahead, he gave the command to lower the house lights. The lights in the theater dimmed, then blacked out. The orchestra began the overture. At the end of the overture, Timmers cued the rope man to raise the curtain on the opening scene, the municipal orphanage.

The sets in *Annie* were massive and required a careful plan to allow the crew to make set changes as efficiently as possible. For example, at the end of the first scene, flymen raised the orphanage windows, and the beds and door moved offstage on treadmills. At the same time, stagehands pushed other pieces onto the stage so that everything was in motion simultaneously. The cross-movement kept the audience from focusing on individual pieces of scenery being changed, which would have been boring. Thus, while the orphanage set pieces were moving off, the buildings that formed the backdrop for the next scene were rolling on.

Some of the scenes in *Annie* required supporting actors to play multiple roles. For example, during the production number "N.Y.C.," actors appeared, left the stage, changed costume, and reappeared on the street in a new guise, to create the effect that there were a lot of people in the street. There was one problem when staging this scene—the dressing rooms in the Alvin were in the basement. Thus, the actors had to step offstage, race down a staircase, slip on a new wig and costume, and race back up the stairs and onto the stage, appearing calm, collected, and ready to sing.

Annie's Influence

Success is self-feeding on Broadway. The success of the show led to more media coverage. The *New York Times*, the *New York Post*, the *New York Daily News*, *Newsweek*, and the *Today Show* all covered the play. The more publicity the media gave the show, the more tickets were sold. The show revived interest in the traditional musical, one in which a story is told from beginning to end in scenes that feature big production numbers. This type of musical had been popularized by composers and lyricists such as Richard Rodgers and Oscar Hammerstein

(*The King and I*, *Oklahoma!*, *Flower Drum Song*, and *South Pacific*, among other shows) and Alan Jay Lerner and Frederick Loewe (*My Fair Lady* and *Gigi*, among others). The trend continued in the 1960s with shows like *Hello, Dolly!*, *Gypsy*, *Fiddler on the Roof*, *Man of La Mancha*, and *Cabaret*. However, trends began to change in the mid-1960s, and interest in the Broadway musical declined. One reason for this was a change in popular culture. From the 1930s through the first half of the 1960s, the songs from musicals were in the same musical style as songs that were playing on the radio. The songs from the shows became hits themselves. But when rock 'n' roll became popular, the younger theatergoing population's taste in music diverged from the style of songs in musicals. Drawing younger audiences became more difficult. The new trend favored ensemble shows that featured a musical revue approach rather than the story of a single main character. As a result, lyricists and composers of traditional musicals either retired or changed their style. Rock operas like *Hair!* (1968), *Jesus Christ Superstar* (1971), and *Grease* (1972) featured rock 'n' roll songs.

Another new approach to drawing an audience was to focus on sex. Bob Fosse, a choreographer whose style of sexy jazz choreography was to become synonymous with Broadway, was the force behind shows such as *Pippin* and *Chicago*. Stephen Sondheim, who as a boy was a neighbor of Oscar Hammerstein, created "concept musicals" such as *Company*, which follows five couples and explores various aspects of the attempt to find love. These plays generally had ensemble casts and explored different elements of a central subject, combining elements of the Broadway "story" musical with those of a musical revue. Sondheim's musicals were popular, but they didn't have the long runs that earlier grand musicals had had. *Company* ran for 706 performances, and *A Little Night Music* (1976) ran for 600. The height of the Broadway concept musical was reached with Michael Bennett's *A Chorus Line*, which revolves around the travails of a group of dancers auditioning for a part in a Broadway show. The various characters reveal their past histories and ambitions through song and dance. Throughout the 1970s, producers reluctant to take a chance on a new big-budget "book" musical stuck with revivals of shows that had already been successful: *Gypsy*, *My Fair Lady*, *Hello, Dolly!*, and *The King and I*. *Annie*'s success and its six-year run demonstrated that the traditional musical was not dead. According to Martin Charnin in *Annie: A Theatre Memoir*, he received thank yous from a number of lyricists and composers of classic musicals. He wrote:

> **The Jerry Hermans and Alan Jay Lerners and Richard Rodgers of the world were saying … "You brought the musical theatre back. You brought the musical comedy back."**

The Broadway show was followed by a national tour in which two troupes crossed the United States, performing the show in various cities. One started in Chicago and the other in Los Angeles. The touring companies brought *Annie* to an ever-larger audience. The play's success revitalized

High school and amateur theater groups around the world frequently find *Annie* an appealing show to perform.

the comic strip *Little Orphan Annie*, as well. The strip was still syndicated in the mid-1970s, but it had been dropped by a number of newspapers. The musical revived interest in the comic strip, bringing the relationship full circle. In addition, the play spawned a wide range of tie-in products. There were Annie toys and dolls, Annie mugs, Annie T-shirts and belts, patterns for dresses, and Annie jewelry, including an Annie locket, among other items. A week after *Annie* opened, Columbia Records recorded the original cast album of the show.

Keeping the Show Going

Even after the show opened, Martin Charnin continued to check on it from time to time, to make sure that the actors were still performing with the energy that would keep the show fresh. Once the show settled in for its run on Broadway, publicity sessions were scheduled at times that allowed the children to attend school in the morning, in order to give them a regular schedule and a sense of stability.

Charnin was a key figure in nineteen productions of *Annie* in New York, in foreign countries, and on national tours. Although the story of *Annie* remained the same, the productions all brought their own unique elements to the story. According to Charnin, with every performance there are different actors, bringing their own interpretation of the roles and the reading of their lines. In addition, each production has its own version of the sets. Each designer has a unique vision that influences the tone of the play. For Charnin, this is what keeps the show alive: it is always changing.

Chapter 4

Revivals, Sequels, and the Movies

*A*nnie's story didn't end with its Broadway run. The show spawned sequels on the stage and in movies and books, not to mention a wide range of tie-in products.

Martin Charnin, Charles Strouse, and Thomas Meehan attempted a sequel to *Annie* in 1989. The play, *Annie 2: Miss Hannigan's Revenge*, focused on the character of Miss Hannigan rather than Annie. This proved to be a mistake. When the show opened at the John F. Kennedy Center for the Performing Arts in Washington, DC, in December 1989, all the reviews were negative. The show's creators made extensive changes to the score and script but eventually decided to call an end to the project. Martin Charnin attributes the show's failure to the mistake of focusing on

Opposite: A scene from the 2012 thirty-fifth-anniversary revival of *Annie*

Miss Hannigan. What audiences wanted was the further adventures of Annie, and they were disappointed. The trio rewrote the play as a continuation of the story begun in the original *Annie*, calling it *Annie Warbucks*. The show was developed at the Goodspeed Opera house as a workshop project, and it was performed Off-Broadway at the Variety Arts Theatre in New York, where it ran for two hundred performances over nine months in 1992–1993.

In 1997, the show's creators attempted a Broadway revival in honor of the twentieth anniversary of *Annie*. The show opened at the Martin Beck Theatre (now the Al Hirschfeld Theatre), starring Nell Carter, a black actress, as Miss Hannigan. The actress who played Annie kept changing. Initially, a well-publicized nationwide search for an actress to play Annie was launched, sponsored by the department store Macy's. It resulted in the casting of twelve-year-old Joanna Pacitti, who was crowned by the original Annie, Andrea McArdle herself, on a special edition of ABC's TV show *Turning Point*. Weeks before the show was due to open, however, Pacitti was fired because of the producers' dissatisfaction with her performance and her lack of chemistry with the actor playing Daddy Warbucks. She was replaced by Brittny Kissinger, who was playing one of the other orphans. When Kissinger developed bronchitis, Alexandra Keisman, yet another orphan, was substituted for her, and she continued in the role. The continual changing of actresses stirred up controversy and bad publicity as the public sympathized with Pacitti. More bad publicity was

THE LONGEST-RUNNING MUSICAL

According to *Playbill*, the following is the list of longest-running musicals on Broadway as of early September 2017. The number after the title is the number of performances. Plays still running at that time are marked with an asterisk.

1. *The Phantom of the Opera**, 12,318
2. *Chicago** (1996 revival), 8,643
3. *The Lion King**, 8,246
4. *Cats*, 7,485
5. *Les Misérables*, 6,680
6. *A Chorus Line*, 6,137
7. *Oh! Calcutta!* (1976 revival), 5,959
8. *Wicked**, 5,779
9. *Mamma Mia!*, 5,773
10. *Beauty and the Beast*, 5,461

Annie is tied with *Cabaret* (1998 revival) with 2,377 performances, as the twenty-sixth longest-running show.

In the 1997 revival of *Annie*, actress Nell Carter became the first black Miss Hannigan.

How *Annie* Made It to the Stage

generated by a series of commercials featuring not Nell Carter, but a white actress, Marcia Lewis, as Miss Hannigan. The producers stated that they had made the commercials during a previous production and it would have been extremely expensive to make new ones. Nell Carter was quoted in the *New York Post* as suggesting that perhaps racism was involved, and the producers were trying to avoid letting the audience know Miss Hannigan was being played by a black woman. She later issued a statement denying that she had accused the producers of racism, however. The show received mixed reviews and closed in October 1997 after 239 performances. However, its short Broadway run was followed by a successful national tour. Nell Carter continued in the role of Miss Hannigan for the first three months of that tour. In January 1998, Carter was replaced by a white actress, Sally Struthers, who played the role for the remainder of the tour.

Anniversary Revival

That was not the last time *Annie* was seen on Broadway, however. In 2012, a thirty-fifth anniversary production of the show was staged on Broadway. For this version, Thomas Meehan revised the musical, and Tony-Award-winning director James Lapine directed. Katie Finneran starred as Miss Hannigan. As in the earlier revival, Lapine conducted a nationwide search for an actress to play Annie, and Lilla Crawford won the role. Meehan said that one reason he chose to revive the play and got backing from several producers was that the United States was suffering an economic downturn at the time, and although it wasn't the Great Depression, it still meant hard times. Reviving *Annie* was a way of giving the public a note of optimism.

Lapine had never seen the show, so his approach was different from that of the original production. He likes realism in his productions, and his revival was grittier than the earlier versions. His *Annie*, which cost $12 million to produce, opened at the Palace Theatre in November 2012. Again, it received mixed reviews. Charnin disliked it, feeling that it took the heart and truth out of the show. The production closed in January 2014 after 487 performances. The producers decided not to mount a national tour of the thirty-fifth anniversary revival, possibly because they feared this version would not be any more popular on the road than it was in New York. Instead, Martin Charnin, now eighty years old, stepped into the breach at the behest of Troika Entertainment, a company that produces road tours of plays. He agreed to direct a road tour of *Annie* based on his original version of the play. Charnin stated that he wanted to "return to the indefinable kind of magic and charm that has long been a part of the show's performances and staging." He angered some of those involved in the revival by saying that much of the humor, heart, and joy present in the original version of the play were missing from the revival much of the time. Despite objecting to Charnin's comments on the revival, Charles Strouse and Thomas Meehan joined Charnin in mounting the version used in the road tour with a production that captured the tone of the original version of the musical. The road tour even included

"TOMORROW"

There are a number of popular songs from Annie, but the most iconic is "Tomorrow," the first song written for the show. The idea for the song originated with Martin Charnin. According to Charnin, the song was written in response to what was happening in the United States in the 1970s. The political situation, the war in Vietnam, and the economy were all problems. Many people were feeling desperate, and even more were disenchanted with the government. Charnin wanted a song that would display Annie's optimistic spirit in the face of overwhelming adversity and express the theme of the play. The song's first line, "The sun will come out tomorrow," captures her attitude perfectly. According to Charnin, once that song was in place, the structure of the play fell into place around it. Annie's attitude focused the way that the scenes were written. Charnin has pointed out that, although the song is very simple, it resonates with people. Often the audience joins Annie in singing the song. "Tomorrow" has been used in commercials, including a Kellogg's cereal commercial in which the original Annie, Andrea McArdle, sings the song, and in an ad by pharmaceutical company Novartis for its drug Entresto, which is used to treat heart failure.

some of the original choreography by Peter Gennaro, restaged by Peter's daughter, Liza Gennaro. In addition, the road tour version featured redesigned costumes and sets rather than using those from the 2012 revival.

The new set was designed by Tony Award–nominee Beowulf Boritt, and Suzy Benzinger was hired as costume designer to create new versions that harkened back to those originally created by Theoni Aldredge (who had died). Bill Berloni, who had provided the dogs for both the original version and the 2012 revival, did so for the tour as well.

Welcome to the Movies

In 1979, Charnin, Meehan, and Strouse sold the movie rights for *Annie* to Columbia Pictures, which released the film in 1982. The producer was Ray Stark, who had produced the movie version of the musical *Funny Girl*. The director was Oscar-winner John Huston. Stark was a commercially focused producer. He wanted to garner as big an audience as possible, and he felt that the story as portrayed in the play wouldn't appeal to the large teenage audience for movies. Therefore, although Thomas Meehan had already been hired to write the screenplay, Stark paid him a large sum to agree to let someone else do it. In fact, he insulted Meehan by making the offer without even bothering to read his script. Stark made a number of changes. Feeling that the play lacked conflict because Daddy Warbucks was so lovable, he instead made Warbucks a tough businessman with no room in his life for children or love. He also created a situation that put Annie into serious peril. The movie

The cast gathers for a celebration in this scene from the 1982 film version of *Annie*.

starred Albert Finney as Oliver Warbucks, Carol Burnett as Miss Hannigan, and Broadway stars Bernadette Peters as Lily and Tim Curry as Rooster. To cast the character of Annie, talent scout Garrison True and his assistants visited twenty cities over ten months and auditioned eight thousand little girls. They finally chose Aileen Quinn, who had played one of the orphans in the Broadway production.

The on-location portion of the film was shot over six weeks on the grounds of Monmouth College (now

Monmouth University) in Long Branch, New Jersey. The college library is housed in the Murry Guggenheim House, which was used for a scene in which Warbucks's helicopter lands on the White House lawn, and a second mansion on the campus, Shadow Lawn, served as Warbucks's home. The New York street scenes and orphanage footage were shot on the Columbia studio back lot in Los Angeles. Several songs were changed, as was some of the plot. The most significant change was switching from a Christmas-themed show to one focused on the Fourth of July. The change was motivated not by dramatic consideration, but by the fact that the locations at Monmouth College were only available during the summer, since they were needed by the college during the school year. With the movie being shot in the summer, it was considered too difficult to get snow.

Charnin, Meehan, and Strouse were so thrilled at the financial offer Columbia made them for the movie rights, that they signed a contract that left them with no say in how the company produced the film. In an interview in the *Hollywood Reporter*, Charnin said, "We foolishly gave up the right to maintain any supervision on the 1982 movie. The money was so extraordinary, it was [my own] selfishness to allow it." Procter & Gamble ran an Annie-related promotion in conjunction with the movie, giving away posters with soap in supermarkets around the country. Coca-Cola's fountain division gave away Annie-themed cups in fast-food restaurants and movie theaters. Despite the publicity, the film garnered a lukewarm response at the box office, earning only about $30 million in the United States,

SHOT IN THE DARK

The filming of the 1982 movie required a change in New Jersey's child labor law, which prohibited children in films from working between 11:30 p.m. and 7:00 a.m. Because Annie's climactic scene had to be shot on the Passaic River's NX railroad drawbridge at night and would take many hours to shoot, Governor Brendan Byrne flew by helicopter to the set to sign a bill amending the law.

and although it received a number of Golden Globe and Oscar nominations, it failed to win any awards. Columbia made $10 million in television rights from both NBC and HBO, as well as millions of dollars more from licensing fees for a wide range of Annie-themed products, so the film was a financial success nonetheless.

A sequel to the movie, *Annie: A Royal Adventure!*, appeared on TV in 1995. It was not a musical and contained no songs other than "Tomorrow." The movie is set some years after the 1982 film. In it, Oliver Warbucks and twelve-year-old Annie pay a visit to England, where Warbucks is to be knighted by the king. Accompanying them are Annie's friends Hannah and Molly. In England, the girls become embroiled in the plot of an evil noblewoman, Lady Edwina Hogbottom, who plans to blow up Buckingham Palace and the heirs to the throne while Warbucks is being knighted. The film was released on DVD in 2004.

A more successful made-for-TV movie of *Annie*, using the original story, was produced by The Walt Disney

Company for its TV series *The Wonderful World of Disney*. The show, broadcast in 1999, was directed by Rob Marshall. Victor Garber played Daddy Warbucks, Kathy Bates was Miss Hannigan, and Alicia Morton was Annie. The movie was a hit, drawing 26.3 million viewers. It won an Emmy Award and a George Foster Peabody Award. It was released on VHS and DVD in 2000.

New Setting

In January 2011, actor Will Smith announced plans to do a remake of the *Annie* movie. The movie, set in the present day, was coproduced with his wife, Jada Pinkett Smith, and rapper Jay-Z. It was released in 2014 by Columbia Pictures (now part of Sony Entertainment). Originally, the film was slated to star the Smiths' daughter, Willow. However, she was too old for the role by the time the movie was actually filmed. Instead, the role of Annie was play by Academy Award–nominated child star Quvenzhané Wallis. Jamie Foxx played an updated version of Daddy Warbucks, named Will Stacks, and Cameron Diaz played Miss Hannigan. The film's song score consisted of most of the original film's songs plus new compositions by Greg Kurstin and Sia.

This version of the story is set in the Harlem area of New York City, where Annie Bennett and several other girls live in a foster home with Colleen Hannigan. Hannigan is a resentful former singer and drunk. A note left by Annie's parents saying that they would return, written on a Domoni's restaurant receipt, leads her to spend every Friday outside the restaurant.

Quvenzhané Wallis, as Annie, with Sandy in the 2014 film version

While trying to save a dog from bullies, Annie is prevented from being run over by cell phone mogul William Stacks. After the video of Annie's rescue goes viral, Stacks invites Annie to move in with him, in an effort to boost his popularity. Stacks bonds with Annie, sharing the story of his own humble beginning. Stacks is running for election as mayor, and his manager conspires with Hannigan to arrange for imposters to claim Annie as their daughter for publicity purposes. Annie is kidnapped by the imposters, but Hannigan has second thoughts and tells Stacks of the plot.

Stacks fires his publicity manager, Guy, who masterminded the plot, and rescues Annie by helicopter. Annie is convinced that Stacks was involved in the plan because the kidnappers thought they were being paid by him through Guy. To prove his sincerity to Annie, Stacks quits the mayoral race. Annie helps him and his assistant Grace realize they love each other. Subsequently, Annie announces the establishment of the Stacks Literacy Center, to help children. The cast sings Annie's "Tomorrow."

Despite mostly negative reviews from film critics, the movie was a success at the box office, making more than $133 million worldwide. It received two Golden Globe Award nominations, one for Wallis as Best Actress in a Motion Picture–Comedy or Musical, and one for Best Original Song.

As with the original movie version of *Annie*, Martin Charnin didn't care for the 2014 movie. He felt the story didn't work in a contemporary setting. To Charnin, *Annie* is a Depression-era story, and its language that of the 1930s. Therefore, it was critical to maintain that milieu as an integral part of the show. Charnin felt that by updating the setting, the producers had created a different story, and by changing the story, they had reduced its power and impact.

In 2006, one of the actors who played an orphan in the original Broadway production, Julie Stevens, and her partner, Gil Cates Jr., produced a documentary film, *Life After Tomorrow*. The film reunited over forty women who had played Annie or orphans in *Annie* to explore their experiences as child stars in a hit show.

Life After Tomorrow premiered at the Phoenix Film Festival on March 24, 2006, where it won awards for Best Documentary and Best Director.

As a result of Annie's immense popularity, companies have produced an amazing variety of tie-in products.

Still More Tie-Ins

Like the play, the 1982 movie led to a variety of products. More than fifty companies manufactured *Annie* products that tied in with the movie. Publisher Random House issued a variety of *Annie* books, including a novelization of the play by Thomas Meehan, an Annie activity book, and original

Annie adventure books, such as *Annie Joins the Circus* by James Howe. Knickerbocker Toys produced a line of Annie dolls and a stuffed Sandy dog. Knowles China Company produced collector plates. Sears featured a line of Annie clothes, using Aileen Quinn to model Annie's outfits. Even Sandy got into the act. After the 1982 movie, Sandy was hired to appear in commercials for the dogfood Ken-L-Ration.

Although Annie was unusual in being a successful show based on a comic, it was traditional in its format—a "book" musical that told a story. In this, it was a continuation of a style that harkened back to the grand musicals of the 1950s and early 1960s. Its major influence on future Broadway productions was to confirm that even in the late 1970s there was still an audience for lavish book musicals—which encouraged producers to continue backing them. It also verified that there was an audience for musicals suitable for the whole family, which encouraged companies such as Disney to produce musicals based on their movies. Many of the actresses who played orphans went on to successful singing or acting careers. Among these are Debbie Gibson, Sarah Jessica Parker, and Catherine Zeta-Jones. *Annie* continues to be produced and is popular with community theater and school drama groups, capturing hearts with the story of a heroic eleven-year-old orphan.

Glossary

ALLIES In World War II, the United States, Canada, Britain, Russia, and other countries were allied in the fighting against Germany, Japan, and Italy.

BANE An annoyance or a cause of great distress.

CAMP A highly stylized or exaggerated performance.

CAPITALISM An economic system in which individuals produce, sell, distribute, and invest in goods and services, as opposed to systems in which the government does so.

CARTEL An organization that controls the production and distribution of a product.

CONSPIRE To agree secretly to engage in a wrong or illegal activity.

CONUNDRUM A difficult, confusing situation or question.

CURTAIN CALL When the cast appears onstage at the end of a show to be recognized by the audience for its performance.

DEBUTED Made its first appearance in public.

FEISTINESS Showing a spirited, aggressive attitude.

GOLDEN GLOBE AWARDS Awards given in various categories by the Hollywood Foreign Press Association for excellence in American motion pictures and television.

HOUSE LIGHTS The lights that provide illumination to the seating area rather than the stage of a theater

HUMANISTIC Something that reflects a doctrine centered on human interests or values, one that stresses an individual's dignity and worth.

IMPEACHMENT The removal from office of a president by Congress.

MOUTHPIECE A person who speaks for the someone else; an official or unofficial spokesperson.

NEW DEAL A series of economic and social programs put into place by Franklin D. Roosevelt that included financial support for the unemployed and projects that provided them with paid work. Among them was Social Security.

OVERTURE A medley of music from a musical that serves as an introduction to the show.

PERISCOPE A type of telescope that could be raised above a barrier so that one could see what's ahead without being seen or exposed to danger.

PLUCK The courage and resolve to overcome obstacles.

PRETENTIOUS Putting on airs and acting self-important.

RECONCILE To bring into agreement two or more differing points of view.

REVUE A collection of song and dance acts presented onstage.

STANDING OVATION When the audience stands to applaud at the end of a show to indicate they think the performance was outstanding.

STIPULATION A condition or rule that is demanded as part of an agreement.

SYNDICATE In media, an organization that distributes a creative professional's work to a variety of outlets such as various newspapers or TV stations.

TROUPE A group of actors, dancers, or other entertainers that puts on a play in different locations.

VIABILITY The ability to survive or work successfully.

WHETTED Sharpened, stimulated, or excited one's interest or appetite.

WING An area on either side of the stage where actors can stand or props and set pieces can be placed prior to being brought onstage.

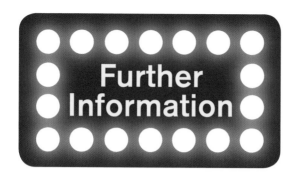

Further Information

BOOKS

Charnin, Martin. *Annie: A Theatre Memoir.* New York: E.P. Dutton, 1977.

Gray, Harold. *Arf! The Life and Hard Times of Little Orphan Annie, 1935–1945.* New York: Arlington House, 1970.

———. *The Complete Little Orphan Annie Volume 1.* San Diego, CA: Library of American Comics, 2008.

Meehan, Thomas. *Annie: An Old-Fashioned Story.* New York: Macmillan, 1980.

ONLINE ARTICLES

Jones, Chris. "Director Martin Charnin: Latest 'Annie' Looks to Past." *Chicago Tribune*, November 5, 2014, http://www. chicagotribune.com/entertainment/theater/ct-martin-charnin-annie-musical-tour-column.html.

Rizzo, Frank. "Annie: Martin Charnin Looks Back at 1976 Goodspeed Premiere." *Hartford Courant*, June 3, 2011, http://articles.courant.com/2011-06-03/features/hc-frank-rizzo-annie-0603_1_goodspeed-opera-house-goodspeed-musical-annie.

Trinchero, Brisa. "Musical Moment: An Interview with Book Writer, Thomas Meehan." MakeMusicals.com. February 21, 2011 http://makemusicals.com/2011/02/musical-moment-an-interview-with-book-writer-thomas-meehan.

VIDEOS

Annie [1977] The Original Cast Performs a Medley on the Tony Awards

https://www.youtube.com/watch?v=ZU2ZaaDQOag

The original Broadway cast of *Annie* performs numbers fromhe show at the 1977 Tony Awards.

Annie—Four Broadway Stars, Andrea McArdle, Sarah Jessica Parker, 1982 TV

https://www.youtube.com/watch?v=GDSZsy191m0

Martin Charnin talks about *Annie* and introduces four stars who played Annie on Broadway.

Annie Songwriters Charles Strouse and Martin Charnin Sit Down at the Piano to Share Tales of Their Iconic Score

http://www.broadway.com/videos/154412/annie-songwriters-charles-strouse-and-martin-charnin-sit-down-at-the-piano-to-share-tales-of-their-iconic-score

The composer and lyricist discuss creating *Annie*.

Writing *Annie* the Musical in [the] 1970s

https://www.youtube.com/watch?v=Zl4FqknviNc

Thomas Meehan, Martin Charnin, and Charles Strouse discuss creating *Annie*.

BOOKS

Aylesworth, Thomas G. *Broadway to Hollywood.*
New York: Gallery Books, 1985.

Bordman, Gerald. *American Musical Theatre: A Chronicle.*
New York: Oxford University Press, 2001.

Bunnett, Rexton S., Michael Patrick Kennedy, and John
Muir. Collins Guide to Musicals. Glasgow, Scotland:
HarperCollins, 1997.

Charnin, Martin. *Annie: A Theatre Memoir.* New York: E.P.
Dutton, 1977.

Gottfried, Martin. *Broadway Musicals.* New York: Harry N.
Abrams, 1979.

Mordden, Ethan. *One More Kiss: The Broadway Musical in
the 1970s.* New York: Palgrave Macmillan, 2003.

Nachman, Gerald. *Broadway's Showstoppers!* Chicago, IL:
Chicago Review Press, 2017.

Viertel, Jack. *The Secret Life of the American Musical: How
Broadway Shows Are Built.* New York: Farar, Straus,
Giroux, 2016.

ONLINE ARTICLES

Associated Press. "'Little Orphan Annie' Cartoon to Disappear From Funny Pages After 86 Years." *Fox News*, June 14, 2010. http://www.foxnews.com/entertainment/2010/06/14/little-orphan-annie-cartoon-disappear-funny-pages-years.html.

"Biography." CharlesStrouse.com, accessed August 22, 2017. http://www.charlesstrouse.com.

Caitlin, Roger. "Depressed by the news? 'Annie's' creator explains why one song still resonates." *Washington Post*, March 12, 2016. https://www.washingtonpost.com/entertainment/theater_dance/depressed-by-the-news-annies-creator-explains-why-one-song-still-resonates/2016/03/10/1f8cfea8-e22e-11e5-9c36-e1902f6b6571_story.html?utm_term=.2a41436ef979.

Cronin, Brian. "Comic Book Legends Revealed #331." CBR.com, September 9, 2011.. http://www.cbr.com/comic-book-legends-revealed-331.

Ferri, Josh. "Annie Yesterday, Today and 'Tomorrow': All About Broadway's Favorite Little Orphan." Broadway.com, October 27, 2012. http://www.broadway.com/buzz/165051/annie-yesterday-today-and-tomorrow-all-about-broadways-favorite-little-orphan.

Grimes, William. "David Mitchell, Broadway Set Designer, Dies at 79." *New York Times*, October 4, 2011. http://

www.nytimes.com/2011/10/05/theater/david-mitchell-broadway-set-designer-dies-at-79.html?mcubz=1.

Healy, Patrick. "Tour's Director Criticizes New 'Annie.'" *New York Times*, February 24, 2014. https://www.nytimes.com/2014/02/26/theater/tours-director-criticizes-new-annie.html?mcubz=1.

Hetrick, Adam. "Martin Charnin Takes Helm of New Annie Tour; Recent Broadway Revival Shelved." *Playbill*, February 24, 2014. http://www.playbill.com/article/martin-charnin-takes-helm-of-new-annie-tour-recent-broadway-revival-shelved-com-215245.

Kelly, Kate. "Little Orphan Annie the Comic Strip." America Comes Alive. Accessed August 7, 2017. http://americacomesalive.com/2014/07/08/little-orphan-annie-comic-strip.

_____. "Sandy, the Canine Star of Broadway's Little Orphan Annie." America Comes Alive. Accessed August 7, 2017. http://americacomesalive.com/2014/07/08/sandy-canine-star-broadways-little-orphan-annie.

"Little Orphan Annie." National Radio Hall of Fame. Accessed August 7, 2017. http://www.radiohof.org/little_orphan_annie.htm.

"Martin Charnin." Masterworks Broadway. Accessed August 10, 2017. http://masterworksbroadway.com/artist/martin-charnin-2.

Radio Archives. "Little Orphan Annie." Accessed August 7, 2017. http://www.radioarchives.com/Little_Orphan_Annie_p/ra005.htm

Rothstein, Mervyn. "Sandy, Mutt Who Made It on Broadway, Dies at 16." *New York Times*, August 30, 1990. http://www.nytimes.com/1990/08/30/theater/sandy-mutt-who-made-it-on-broadway-dies-at-16.html?mcubz=1.

Sanford, James. "A Comics History of Little Orphan Annie." BirthDeathMovies, October 30, 2014. http://birthmoviesdeath.com/2014/10/30/a-history-of-annie.

Schwartz, A. Brad. "American Children Faced Great Dangers in the 1930s, None Greater Than 'Little Orphan Annie.'" Smithsonian.com, December 15, 2015. http://www.smithsonianmag.com/history/american-children-faced-great-dangers-1930s-none-greater-little-orphan-annie-180957544.

"The Sun Will Come Out Tomorrow: Thomas Meehan on the Importance of Writing Optimistic Themes in *Annie*, *Hairspray*, *The Producers* and his other musicals." *Columbus Dispatch*, August 27, 2013. http://www.dispatch.com/article/20130827/blogs/308279712.

Turan, Kenneth. "Hollywood Puts Its Money on Annie." *New York Times Magazine*, May 2, 1982, http://www.nytimes.com/1982/05/02/magazine/hollywood-puts-its-money-on-annie.html?pagewanted=all&mcubz=1.

Williams, Christian. "Rights! Bankers! 'Annie!'" *Washington Post*, June 19, 1982. https://www.washingtonpost. com/archive/lifestyle/1982/06/19/rights-bankers-annie/ b9020a43-de5e-49f5-8803-165690c7b4f6/?utm_term=. ad5c423a395a.

VIDEO

"Annie Songwriters Charles Strouse and Martin Charnin Sit Down at the Piano to Share Tales of Their Iconic Score." Broadway.com, posted November 3, 2012. http://www. broadway.com/videos/154412/annie-songwriters-charles-strouse-and-martin-charnin-sit-down-at-the-piano-to-share-tales-of-their-iconic-score.

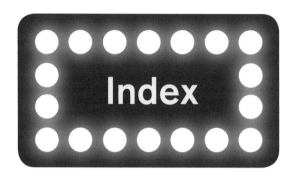

Index

Page numbers in **boldface** are illustrations.

About the Author

JERI FREEDMAN has a bachelor of arts degree from Harvard University. She is the past director of the Boston Playwrights' Lab, an organization that produced original plays in Boston, Massachusetts. Her play *Uncle Duncan's Delusion* was published by Baker's Plays (now part of Samuel French), and her play *Choices*, co-written with Samuel Bernstein, was staged at the American Theatre of Actors in New York City. She is also the author of more than fifty young-adult nonfiction books, including *Exploring Theater: Stage Management in the Theater* and *Exploring Theater: Directing in the Theater*.